An Ozark Odyssey

An Ozark Odyssey

Poems and Essays by
Tom Whiteside

August House / Little Rock

FIRST EDITION 1985

International Standard Book Number 0-935304-95-9

Library of Congress Cataloging in Publication Data

Whiteside, Tom, 1901-

    An Ozark Odyssey

    1. Ozark Mountains — Poetry.   I. Title.
PS3573.H488209 1985   811'.54   85-70447
ISBN 0-935304-95-9

This book and other August House books may be purchased by schools, libraries, churches and other groups and organizations who wish to resell the book as a fund-raising activity. For specific information about this plan, write the Director of Special Promotions at the address above.

Cover painting by Troy Anderson.
Illustrations by Troy Anderson.
Book design by Ted Parkhurst.
Production artwork by Byron Taylor.

Dedicated to the memory of
my father and mother

William Jacob Whiteside
1869-1951

Nora Trammell Whiteside
1876-1959

Contents

Introduction

This is hardly the age of epic poems, but Tom Whiteside, whose life parallels the twentieth century, has, in effect, written his own — not to honor himself, but to share the experiences and discoveries of his personal journey through this turbulent period. Because Tom Whiteside is a man of rare vision, generous spirit, and sound wisdom as well as a poet with distinctive gifts, the results are enriching and memorable.

Those who enjoyed his first two volumes, *Along Sager Creek* (1982) and *An Inland Journey* (1983), will find *An Ozark Odyssey* the fitting climax to this modern-day epic. Although Tom Whiteside undoubtedly has more poetry to write, his major theme has been established: It is our urgent need in this fragmented age to perceive the physical world and the spiritual world in their true relationship to one another, and to delight in both.

The tall oak tree with roots planted deep in the earth and limbs extending skyward often recurs as a metaphor in this poet's work. The motif springs from his own duality of experience: his life stabilized and rooted in his beloved hills of Northwest Arkansas, and his spirit always reaching upward, searching out new territories to explore.

Born of pioneer stock in 1901, in close touch with the history of the region, Tom Whiteside studied at the University of Arkansas during World War I and has lived his adult years as a banker, community leader, and devoted husband and father in "this favored land." But his odyssey consists of much more, for in the autumn of his life, he found his initiation as a poet, and since then he has engaged in a journey of the spirit, moving beyond the seen to what he calls Universal Space and Time, where time is not measured by the sun, and where rhythms of the Universe can be heard. This dimension is often suggested in his work by the motif of the dogwood in bloom.

Those discovering Tom Whitside for the first time will recognize that no matter what their interest, this volume holds something for them. History enthusiasts and those wanting to recreate Northwest Arkansas' pioneer past in the sesquicentennial year will find the first section of *Odyssey* absorbing reading, while smiling at the warmth and humor of these poems. For sheer pleasure the reader is urged not to miss "Ten in 1912" and for a poignant awareness of local history, some time spent in "Monte Ne" is recommended.

The second section of *Odyssey* will wholly engross those who enjoy reading about other lives. It movingly recounts Tom Whiteside's journey of personal growth, his vibrant response to nature, and the challenges faced by a youthful spirit in an aging body. "Editorial Comment," "Certainty," and "The Gift" are choice examples.

The third section will delight poets and lovers of poetry. The author's joy in joining the endless communion of poets who can write with spiritual vision is not diminished by his critical reactions to modern poetry at the abyss. Poets with a sense of purpose will especially savor "New Scenery," "Affirmations," and "As Servant to the Source."

Pervading the entire book is Tom Whiteside's call to faith and individual creativity, a call which is sure to send others off on their own explorations.

Tom Whiteside is that rare poet who has been able to go beyond the craft of words to bring a united meaning out of many single poems so that his work stands as one confession, as one letter to the world.

Happily, we can believe that, like Ulysses, he will go right on exploring — always another voyage and, perhaps, for us, another volume!

Gloria Okes Perkins
Springdale, Arkansas

Part I

I choose to give my testimony
and let it be judged,
that my experiences may be added
to the sum of written records.

My purpose . . . to record
discoveries
of faith and love
as I journey toward wholeness.

My place . . . Northwest Arkansas
beside an Ozark stream
where
tall oaks grow and dogwoods bloom.

AN ODYSSEY OF THE OZARKS

"Tell me, Muse, of that man, so ready at need, who wandered far and wide, after he had sacked the sacred citadel of Troy, and many were the men whose towns he saw and whose mind he learnt, yes, and many the woes he suffered in his heart upon the deep, striving to win his own life and the return of his company."

Homer, *The Odyssey*

Unlike Ulysses, this traveler is an Ozarkian, born in the Ozarks near the beginning of the twentieth century. I never wandered in far lands or sacked the sacred city of Troy. My journey has been an inland journey, deep within myself, moving toward a wholeness I never reach. Yet my striving, like that of Ulysses, has shaped a new life for myself, a new style of life which I would heartily commend to my own grandchildren, and other grandchildren, wherever they may be.

I relate the events of my life as they happened, without fanfare or exaggeration of the age that is forever gone. Like Ulysses, I find this recording necessary, and in one man's search universal values can be found. The setting of my own saga in these beautiful Ozark mountains make events seem almost a growing out of the tall oak trees, dogwood blooms, and clear spring-fed streams that constitute my world.

It is, of course, evident that a ripening process takes place in nature, plants, animals, and human beings. I see that each individual needs to concentrate on the ripening of instincts through knowledge and understanding of culture, tradition, and religion. As an older person I choose to give my testimony and let it be judged, so that my experiences may be added to the sum of written records. My purpose is not to instruct or lecture, but to record discoveries of faith and love, as I journey toward wholeness.

In chronological order, then, I relive my experiences in these Ozark Mountains. I reconstruct my own birth, as told to me. A mother's firstborn, an anxious father, a saddled horse and a hasty trip to town to get the doctor. The doctor coming by horse and buggy on a Monday night in mid-December—after the drought of 1901, a gentle snow falling on the dry, dry ground.

In eighty-two years of living, I consider the events that have taken place—childhood, my occupation, my family, labors as an active member of this century, world wars, depressions, assassinations, and the tragedies of Vietnam and Watergate. Now released from obligations and responsibilities, I seek through poetry in these Ozark Mountains to find the rhythms of the Universe and to let these experiences become the foundation of my life in the now, and in the future.

My mind a collage like pasting on a single surface unassociated experiences, yet all one piece of tapestry, a shifting kaleidoscope of memories. . . .

I remember the romp and play of childhood fun, the mystery of a newborn calf, the gaze into the distant sky of stars, the pursuit of fireflies on the lawn .

I remember the first automobile that came to my community and the first smell of burning gasoline in my young and sensitive nostrils.

In my dim remembering stands the open air chautauqua grounds where twice the Honorable William Jennings Bryan addressed the crowds.

I also remember the first airplane in the neighborhood, the crowds assembled. I can still feel their excitement as well as the

An early scene of the Whiteside home

reaction of cattle and horses in a nearby pasture, snorting through their nostrils as if sensing some great danger.

I remember the first day of school and being taken there by an older cousin, all this arranged by my thoughtful father to give security and confidence on that eventful day.

I remember living on the border near the Indian Nation, now Oklahoma, the wild country becoming civilized, the Trail of Tears, the Battle of Pea Ridge, Judge Parker's Court, all these realities ancient history, but still discussed in my home.

The Civil War was painfully real in my own household—my father's father a Confederate soldier, my mother's mother a Northern sympathizer, and the battle still being fought for my young ears.

I remember my grandfather, a Justice of the Peace, and I became witness to weddings and to courts held in the living room.

I recall the twenty-fourth of June celebration, a big yearly event. I thrilled to the balloon ascensions in the park, the martial music played from the bandstand—ah, I remember the surge within, the quickened step, then the carnival, the politicians speaking, the barkers shouting, and vanilla ice cream dripping from a cone.

I remember standing barefoot in cultivated ground between the rows of corn after a hard rain. The sight and sound and smell synthesized to the feel of warm mud between my toes. I recall

The author's grandparents, L. K. Trammell and Margy LeFors Trammell

picking apples, making apple cider, making ice cream after a hail storm, growing beans and tomatoes for the market, milking cows before and after school. The first telephone, a party line that all my uncles and aunts and cousins were on. And on clear summer nights, the fireflies everywhere, sparkling to the music of crickets, and in the sky Halley's great comet.

As a teen-ager, now thirteen years old, I listened to grownup talk of an ominous nature, and then one day, the news of the sinking of the *Lusitania,* the talk of war.

When sixteen and in college, soldiers on the campus everywhere, influenza, draped windows, the carrying away of the dead. Then while attending class in Old Main in November, the sudden din of whistles blowing, bells ringing—the end of World War One.

I recall in my chosen profession of banking that I attended a convention in Cleveland, Ohio, where President Hoover spoke

Mother Pickens and granddaughter Grayce

about two chickens in every pot and two cars in every garage. I heard dissenters in the park and recoiled when they shouted, "To hell with the President of the United States."

I remember one day when fifty banks in Arkansas closed their doors and the bank panic was on, then the voice of Roosevelt on the radio: "There is nothing to fear but fear itself." After that, the enactment of the F.D.I.C. and business as usual.

I recollect walking to the postoffice for the mail, listening to Hitler haranguing on the radio from loud speakers outside a drug

President Franklin D. Roosevelt and Governor Homer Adkins, April, 1943

store on Main Street, his gospel of hate reverberating up and down the street. I think back to the drought of '34, the hard times continuing, and government men buying cattle for ten dollars a head, then driving them into a gully and shooting them. And before we recovered, the human holocaust in Europe, the Battle of Britain, Churchill on the radio asking for sweat, blood and tears. A neighbor's son leaving home in Uniform.

That quiet Sunday afternoon in December of 1941 when a bulletin crowded out the radio program: "Pearl Harbor has been bombed. All service men are ordered to report to their stations."

Later—much later—Vietnam and war in the living room, instant communication, instant commentary, instant feedback. John Fitzgerald Kennedy ... Martin Luther King ... the beginning of assassinations ... Lyndon Baines Johnson, Richard Milhous Nixon ... Kissinger and Mao-Tse-Tung ... Burning and rioting in the streets of our own country. Then Watergate, as though the grotesque climax of a violent narrative. Then Gerald Ford, Jimmy Carter, and more than three-fourths of the twentieth century is over.

I realize now that there are no representative heroes any more, that no great epic poem can be written for all people, that the American epic cannot be written, but each man must write his

The author's grandfather, James Beaty Whiteside

own. I know that I need the knowledge of history, but it is also my responsibility to make my own history and write my own poetry. I have discovered that each man is born with a sleeping hero within his own unconscious, to be awakened, to develop in an individual way. I believe every person has a journey to take, to fit the unique self in harmony with the rhythms of the Universe.

The great struggle of life is to put these rhythms in harmony, discovering the love that Dante found with instinct and intellect balanced equally as in a wheel whose motion nothing jars.

Well past midway in life's journey, I project a drama into the future, using my imagination, relaxed and at home with myself, my consciousness free from organized delusions, or the projections of personal conflicts.

I build a relationship with my beloved Ozark Mountains. I treat them like a long and trusted friend, and they seem to reciprocate. I use them as a sounding board, letting them speak to me and I to them.

Not unmindful of history and my faith in the Trinity, my imagination becomes a way of lifting myself outside my own skin and my place in nature, so that I can become in harmony with all nature. Sensitive to suffering, I am also free to express joy in the continuity of Life.

It is joy that writes this prayer· "From these Ozark Mountains, O God, I thank You for Your attention. I pray this volume be bound with Your love, as I attempt to speak to the future and to all grandchildren."

THE GREAT MOMENT

Today I watched
A jet plane in the sky
Trailed by vapors in a narrow lane.

And I remembered
When my Uncle Sam and I
Rode to a neighbor's house
In a one-horse buggy
On a gravel lane
When I was only five.

On the way back home
With a twinkle in his eyes
He told me to take the reins and drive.

I was not destined to guide
Screaming jets through the sky.
A pilot
Would never say to me:
"Take the controls and fly."

But no airman
Will taste a greater joy
Than when
I slapped the reins
On Goldie's back
And felt the buggy
Move!

COME BE MY GUEST

Come be my guest in Northwest Arkansas
And watch the sun rise on a mountain stream
And dogwoods bloom beneath a tall oak tree.
Hear the murmur of an Ozark stream
And listen to a mockingbird sing.
Come be my guest
And listen to my story among these hills
About these favored people and their land,
About events well written in the history books
But from my memory as I remember them
Told by my parents, grandparents, and friends.
And let me tell about my long life
In these hills,
From the horse and buggy days
Into the space age.
Then at times I'll talk about my faith
And the nature of the Universe
Beyond all physical space and time—
A new life that has opened up to me.
And if recounting these experiences should
Be helpful in your life
I will be grateful, ever so grateful.

RECORDINGS

I've listened
To the murmur of an Ozark mountain stream.
I've viewed
The blossoms of a dogwood tree on Easter Sunday.
I've tasted
Blueberry pies made from berries grown on an Ozark hill.
I've smelled
The blossoms on a multitude of honeysuckle vines.
I've felt,
With joy, a gentle breeze address the whole of me.
All these have been recorded
Upon my soul
Where substances of greater magnitude reside.

FROM MY OWN CRYSTAL BALL

I cherish most the childhood memory
that can be bidden at my beck and call,
resounding like a distant waterfall
to resurrect a time well known to me:
A secret well of joy destined to be
my own, my own, to treasure and recall,
a spark of life from out a crystal ball,
a vision held within a mystery.

A special one keeps coming to my mind:
of catching fireflies on the lawn at night
with Halley's comet high up in the sky.
O what a joy in my old age to find
myself endowed with faculties to write
these lines and suddenly exclaim—Oh My!

TEN IN 1912

In memory I'll paint the pages on
My calendar and make them new for you,
I'll draw old images upon my mind
From deep within my inner consciousness
And bring to life an age that is no more.
I'll tell my Muse to come and guide the way
Along those childhood paths in Nineteen-Twelve
Through my beloved Ozark hills, and set
The tone in time when life was measured by
The sun, and character was molded in
The home. The Trail of Tears, a civil war,
Judge Parker's Court and hellish border crimes
Still seeded my family's remembrances.
And in a flash I'm near the old homestead
Beneath a maple tree, next to the old
Wellhouse, my heart on fire, and all at once
This spot is made a focal point to quest
For memories. It seems as though my dad
Is standing there to give advice and help
Me in my search. I'm ten years old again
And pumping water in the wooden tank
For thirsty stock—a chore laid down for me
To do before and after school. Again
I feel a fury bursting in my mind
Because, for now, I cannot run and play,
My work mapped out like blueprints on a chart,
With every hour a certain thing to do.
No cars, no telephones, no radios,
No picture shows or TV scenes to watch,
While time moves slow on horse and buggy wheels.

It seems so real to live my past again,
My Muse, with memory so fresh and clear.
Once more, with all those household chores to do,
Like churning cream to make the butter rise.
(It was a chore I hated most of all.)
I never sat and churned like my Aunt Matt
Would do. I stood as angry as a bear,

As agitated as the cream I churned.
I'd slam the dasher up and down inside
The churn and sometimes splash the cream out on
The floor. I was a prisoner tied down
To household duties on the farm, while I
Had boy's jobs waiting for me outside,
Like catching butterflies or swimming
Naked in a nearby stream. Then just as
Regular as the rising/setting sun
The cows must be milked night and morning too.

I never milked a cow tranquilly;
I'd grab a teat and squirt the milk into
The pail. Sometimes the cow would sense my hate
Of milking her and kick the pail from out
My hands and bolt the barn and leave me there
Reflecting on the evils of my day.

But now as I relive those times once more,
I know that character was being made
And supervised by masters of the art,
And love, though not expressed in words as such,
Was evident in every wish and will.
Not every day was made for work. Some days
Were shaped for fun—when friends and families
Were gathered for a singing fest, and then
The time of times when ice-cream suppers were
An added joy. And on each Saturday
A trip to town to buy some needed things.
Not much, for most were grown and stored upon
The farm. Then times I long remember now,
Like catching fire-flies on the lawn at night
And listening to the neighbors talk about
Grown-up events that filled their busy days.
Every Sunday was a special day—
No work except the necessary chores
To do. No other work was ever done.
We'd dress up in our very best and ride
To church in a two-seated buggy with
A fringe on top, all four of us. I'd ride

Up front with Dad, so proud, my mother and
My brother in the back. And even now
Sometimes I hear the sound of horse's hoofs
And steel-rimmed buggy wheels on gravel roads,
And church bells ringing clear and loud. It was
A time of fantasy for me. I'd sit
In church and dream of mansions in the sky.
But change was in the air. In poetry
And human character, with discipline
Erased from rules, the open road would bring
A new beginning to its travelers.

New beginnings are experiences
In every life and I have had my share,
So now I read and audit my long life
And joy to find creation still alive
With all my years to witness life anew.
I too have changed in character like all
The rest since I was ten in Nineteen-Twelve,
But even now when things are not just right
I think of churning cream and milking cows,
Then smile a bit and all my fury's gone.

RETURNING HOME

I went to bed at half-past eight
    And soon I was asleep.
I dreamed I was at home again
    In Nineteen-Hundred-Twelve,
Among my friends and family
    I longed to see once more.
I found them just as they had been,
    A joy to meet and greet.
I saw myself as I once was,
    A joyful lad and free.
Old images began to form
    That almost made me cry—
My pockets full of chin-qua-pins,
    A'whistling as I went.
I took my knife and cut a pole
    From off a sycamore
As I had done so long ago
    And whittled it down to size.
I tied to it a line and hook
    And dug a can of worms.
I took a short-cut through the woods
    Down to a fishing hole.
And after I had caught some fish
    I took off all my clothes
And dived into the swimming hole
    With all my boyhood friends.
Before I woke up from my dream
    I wandered far and near,
My pockets full of chin-qua-pins,
    A'whistling as I went.

THEN AND NOW

Dear Joe Caldwell, Marketing Agent, Benton State Bank:
There's not much I can say in twenty-four lines
about the changes of the last fifty years.
It would take a hundred books and more.
I'm glad you let me write in free verse form.
There's not much rhyme and meter
in all that's been going on.
All I can rightfully tell about in these few lines
are the changes in my income and my automobile;
the rest I leave to your imagination.
My salary way back then
was one hundred dollars per month, AMEN,
no fringe benefits or bonuses.
Never mind the rhyme, it was only accidental.
My automobile was a black Ford coupe,
the one I courted my wife in.
I had to sell it during the depression
and sit on the front porch and watch the world go by.
Now I drive a Regency Oldsmobile,
a joy and delight,
but one hundred dollars a month won't buy the gasoline.
Oh, by the way,
please send me a loan application.
My taxes are coming due.

THE WORLD OF FINANCE,
THE WORLD OF PROSE

"Banking is education. It has to be to survive."

Mary G. Roebling

Some things in life just do not lend themselves to genuine poetry, and my experience in banking is one of them. I had received a full high school education and a more formal education at the University. If I see it as meager now, it is my fault: I did not put my best effort forth! But banking was a different matter altogether. It was my educational institution, my university. It attracted my full attention from the start, and filled my conscious mind with vivid experiences and often times of frustration, conflict, and turmoil.

I know of no environment, no organization, no activity better suited than a bank to teach a person what life in the flesh is really and truly about. Many other bankers have made the same observation. Mary G. Roebling, at 79 the chairperson emeritus of National State Bank in Elizabeth, New Jersey, said this after more than 46 years in banking: "You not only learn about the world of finance, but about the world of politics and the world of sociology and the world of human striving and human success, as well as human failure. . . . Banking is education. It has to be to survive."

Well, the Great Depression taught me about survival, and my institution did survive. If my journey in the material world has traversed the world of banking, that road of conflict has led me to a synthesis and survival. Although my banking experience has not entered directly into my poetry, I am confident that all the incidents of that time reside dormant in my unconscious, ready to be re-experienced in a spontaneous reaction, helping or hindering me at this distant point in my life.

It may even be that every poet needs some experience in the world of prose!

AN ALL-AMERICAN

Some fifty years ago, my love,
    Our wedded days began;
Each day brought forth a greater day,
    A love that grew and grew.

Some days were roller coaster times
    In our amusement park;
We rode into the sky and felt
    A joy that was complete.

All winds were not the gentle kind,
    Some blew hard and cold;
But, like the seasons, spring did come
    To melt our ice and snow.

Although no days would we give back,
    For each has had its place
To meld and mold our family
    Into a solid whole.

The children and grandchildren too
    Pay honor and respect
For all your deeds and loving care:
    You are a royal queen.

This day we proudly title you
    The mother of the year
And place you in our Hall of Fame,
    An All-American.

MY GRANDPA

I come today to stand where you have stood
and hold your presence in my memory,
to resurrect the things you did for me
and offer up my love and gratitude.
You taught me moral strength and fortitude
and how they rule my very destiny.
You taught me that success is mine to be,
while love is of the greatest magnitude.

To all the world you stood four-square and true,
you were a mediator for the peace,
your every wish and will was harmony.
Out of your life our many pleasures grew;
your wisdom in our lives will never cease.
You were the founder of our family.

THE BLUE AND THE GRAY

When war broke out in Sixty-One
There was all hell to pay.
My mama's folks, they chose the Blue;
My papa's folks, the Gray.

Grandma Margy LeFors Trammell
(From on my mama's side)
She never had kind words to say
About the other side.

To her it was a "civil war"—
She'd spit the words out tight;
My papa's folks would say "The War
Between The States" was right.

"They stole my cows and chickens too,"
I'd hear my grandma say,
Her words gathering venom
For all who wore the Gray.

My grandpa on my papa's side
Would chuckle just a bit
While all of us held our breath—
He was our favorite.

"Pass the beans to that old rebel,"
(Motioning with her thumb)
"Before he starts another war—
That mean old rascal bum."

My grandpa on my papa's side,
He'd look as if to think
Before he filled his plate with beans
And gave me one broad wink.

Now I understand:
My grandma was quite tame
And with a captive audience
She only played a game.

A PEA RIDGE BATTLE TALE

Come join me now and you will hear
A Pea Ridge battle tale.
You'll travel on the Old Wire Road,
A famous wartime trail.

At Elkhorn Tavern you will hear
The natives tell their view
Of how it was along the trail
In Eighteen-Sixty-Two.

You'll hear what each side had to say—
The Blue and the Gray—
And give to each their due and be
Observer to the fray.

Then sort the fact and fancies out
To read the story true,
And then you'll hear the battle sounds
As though they were brand-new.

You'll listen to the folklore tales
And what they had to say
About two guineas brought from Georgia
To keep the snakes away.

You'll hear a native woman's tale:
(Her words will make you cry)
"My ears have heard the cannons roar,
I've seen a soldier die.

"My home close to the battlefield
And me a little girl,
A soldier killed in my backyard—
I saw him twist and whirl.

"Bushwhackers came to rob and kill,
The law their own to bid,
I saw them torture my own kin
To tell of treasures hid."

You'll stand beside an old rail fence
In thin and frigid air
On ground where battle lines were formed
And picture yourself there.

You'll hear again the dry cornstalks
Rattling in the field
And walk full length along
A Pea Ridge battlefield.

You'll eat parched corn and sowbelly
In tents threadbare and torn,
You'll travel pathways in the hills
In a patched uniform.

One day you'll hear the cannon roar,
And then a cannon ball
Will set a tall oak trembling
As tree limbs shake and fall.

You'll see two soldiers fall at once,
One wearing Blue; one, Gray;
And right before you, their blood
Commingling in the clay.

And then you'll see the battle end
On a gloomy Saturday,
The snow and slush, the blood and wounds,
The South in disarray.

McCulloch, McIntosh, and Slack,
All three laid to rest—
A western Gettysburg. The South
Has lost its very best.

The Union under Curtis won
The battle of the ridge
And caused Missouri State to own
A northern heritage.

You'll watch old Elkhorn Tavern burn,
Flames reaching for the sky,
You'll walk alone along Wire Road
And wonder, wonder why!

You've traveled on Old Wire Road
And seen the soldiers die
And heard what Mother Pickens said
In words that make one cry.

And now, some wiser than before
Along these battle trails,
You'll end your trip into the past,
Assured that calm prevails.

When winter once again has passed
And green is everywhere
You'll travel through the tended park
And breathe the peaceful air.

In apple blossom time you'll stand
On Old Wire Road and pray
To heal the wounds engendered here
By both the Blue and Gray.

Along the way you'll see that oak
The cannon ball had found,
And you'll be filled with joy to know
It stands mature and sound.

With Blue and Gray blood in your veins,
You'll come to view and hail
An Elkhorn Tavern built anew
And tell a Pea Ridge Tale.

You'll fancy where the battle raged
On top a rugged hill
Where blended blood, the Blue and Gray,
Returned to nature's till.

To let the blossoms share their view
For all the world to gain,
You'll joy to see them rendezvous
When dogwoods bloom again.

DRAMA IN THESE HILLS . . .

Takes me back in time
O memory
To the Trail of Tears, Judge Parker's Court,
The Pea Ridge Battle, a western Gettysburg,
Coin Harvey's Monte Ne,
and hell upon the border.

J. William Fulbright and Orvil Faubus,
Both Ozarkians
Growing up in these hills
Within thirty miles of one another.

A Hollywood production was filmed
In Northwest Arkansas:
The producers talked of our wonderful
People and our land,
But filmed a drama about other states.

Paradox, O Paradox.

MONTE NE

I stood alone one day upon the banks
Of Beaver Lake not far from my home town
In Benton County, Arkansas, to view
A favored spot and let my thoughts recall
A town that is no more, a village known
Both far and near as Monte Ne. I came
A penitent with troubled heart to draw
A picture of the past and meditate
In silence on events and things that used
To be. I stood and watched the white caps rise
And fall upon the turbid lake, each one
A mindless splash. My ears were filled with noise
Of sloshing water on its shores as though
It were the burdens pounding on my sad
And troubled soul. An early frost had touched
The leaves of maple, sassafras, and gum,
And suddenly old views came back to me
To freshen all my memories of how
Things used to be before the dam was built
And Monte Ne was still a town—to think
Of nature and its joys, commingling with
The thought of man's disturbing role in it
And how to meet the needs of men and still
Preserve the order of the universe.
To questions just like these, I know I must
Address my feeling and my intellect
So I may measure all the good and bad
And be forever faithful to the truth:
To know that out of nature man has weaved
His way and sometimes gutted it as though
A thief, yet sometimes made the flowers bloom
Where land was rough and only brambles grew.
So let me speak of man and his own kind
Who likewise love the valleys and the lakes.

While standing there, I heard an inland voice:
It told of William H. "Coin" Harvey's dream
To build a city in the Ozark hills

That would survive the evils of the world.
His argument was silver versus gold
And William Jennings Bryan, candidate
For President, had been his silver voice
And caused his books to sell. He thought the world
Was damned and due to die. Yet, on this day
As I look out on captured water in
The lake, there is no trace of monument
Or town. I'm told that more than fifty feet
Of water hides the town and countryside.
It was a man's event when water came,
Another's dream against "Coin" Harvey's dream
To fill and overflow, no matter what
The cost to vegetation and the trees.
You can presume it was a peaceful day
Without a sign of rain. Was it in spring?
Were dogwood trees in bloom? Oh, tell! Oh, tell!
Were robins nesting in the maple trees?
Had all the tall oak trees been cut and hauled
Away? Was there a ragged doll named Ann
Somewhere in an abandoned house? Were all
The kittens safe and sound? Does someone know
How many animals were roaming on
The land that day when fishes came to take
Their place. Did they rush in and swish their tails
When first they viewed the streets of Monte Ne?
Did they establish law and order there
To rule and govern over them? And now
With notions like these rambling in my mind
I let my thoughts undo all local time
And stand alone in time and out of time
(Of time before the dam was built and time
Unraveled yet in time) reflecting on
The wisdom or evils of the dam,
And if someday the dam should break and spill
Its water flowing in the waiting streams
And leave to view the streets of Monte Ne
And the remains of old "Coin" Harvey's dream
Where these last years the fishes swam in droves
And once the children came to run and play.

But who am I to say what's right or wrong
For I was born to man and nature too;
Or say that man has failed and caused a town
And countryside to die. This treatise comes
To witness all and tell of beauty lost
And beauty gained and joy engendered there.
O Man! O Nature! Each with restless lives,
I long to find a way to heal your wounds.
For I am man, also, in nature born.

FAYETTEVILLE

Fayetteville, old Fayetteville
Queen city of the Ozarks
The home of Archibald Yell
And the University.
I stand in memory
Near Old Main on the campus
As names cross through my mind
Bill Fulbright and Bob Leflar
Crip Hall and Brooks Hays
Deacon Frazier and John Smith
Stubby Robinson and Ernest Bunch
Stitz Hays and "Bags" Smith
George Blodget and Jim Rutherford
Hugh Feemster and Chester Clardy
Names I knew as undergraduates.
Then one day in class in Old Main
The bells are ringing and whistles blowing
And World War One is over.
Then I catch a glimpse
Of Winkleman's rooming house
On Dixon Street in Nineteen-Eighteen,
Gray Hall and Jeff Hall—
One for sleeping, one for bathing
And nearby Hill Hall for eating.
Now I must report
An era is forever gone.
I leave to you
To fill events with meanings
And these names to their destiny.

BROOKS HAYS

Conviction took hold of you
at an early age.
Responsibility grew out of your experience
Humor in you was inborn.
When a senior student in Nineteen-Nineteen
at the University of Arkansas,
you were cited by the Board of Trustees
for "recent disturbances"
and suspended three days
for participating in a "student rebellion."
Even then you showed compassion
and spoke in mild tones.
Conviction, responsibility, humor,
and a long and fateful career
was to make you one of Arkansas's
best beloved native sons. No doubt
history will record this fact
and your life will be a continuous example
for other good men.

While little men were scuttling here and there
you stood upright,
greater than your own party.
You were a statesman
made so by deep resolutions.
Your day of defeat
was in reality a day of victory.
You were a man of faith
with foundations deeper than yourself.
You held a firm commitment
to the democratic tradition.
You had this to say:
"Our public school system
must be preserved.
Without it the freedom that flowers
from an educated citizenry would perish."
You also said:
"The door that religion alone can open

leads to a pure passageway
of peace and justice."

You described your long and happy life
as living in five worlds
and in your usual humorous way:
"A hotbed of tranquility."
As you so eloquently described others,
at times you were describing yourself.
It was your idea of identification
that every truly happy person
identifies with the peoples of every race;
as you reported in your book:
"The calm and internally peaceful person"
is one "who finds his contentment
in relating his laughter and his tears
to the needs and aspirations
of the peoples
of this restless world."
You truly became as you wished,
happily identified with your family,
your church,
and with the entire human family.

You were caught in the seething
cauldron of emotion in your time and place.
The crisis of your life
as well as the crisis
of your state and nation
came at the height of your career.
You were already established
in your five worlds.
You were recognized
for your training and abilities in law.
You had served several years
as a distinguished member of Congress.
You were recognized and loved
as a layman in the Baptist Church.
You were prominent
in the social work of your state and nation.

If calm had prevailed
you would, no doubt,
have lived in peace and tranquility
the remainder of your life.

But that was not meant to be.
A huge time bomb was in place and ticking
in your state and in the nation.
Many knew about the bomb
but no one knew it was destined
to explode in your state, and so alter your life.
The most knowledgeable expected it to happen
in the Carolinas, Kentucky, or Virginia.
But local events and personalities
caused it to happen in Arkansas:
a governor, a newspaper, and a black leader—
each with decided opinions of what was right.
(At this late date and in keeping with the spirit
and the character of our hero, the author
will not relate any of the stated charges
so often discussed, pertaining to
and regulated by the expediency
of the participating parties.)
The future is our responsibility,
so let us resolve to heal the wounds of this event.

ONLY YESTERDAY

Only yesterday
the birds were singing
in the forty acres of woods
just outside the city.
If you had wandered by
you would have noticed
squirrels at play
and here and there
a patch of wildflowers in bloom.

That was
before the deeds were signed
to subdivide
and the bulldozers
were filled with gasoline
and moved in
to pull down the trees
and build streets where they stood.

I wonder
if someone
wandering down these streets
that once were woods
will someday pause
where I stand now
to see the view
and joy to find
a patch of wildflowers
some thoughtful person
has planted
and catch the sound
of singing birds.

RECOUNTING HISTORY

I've stood there on the ground near Plymouth Rock
Where the Pilgrims are said to have landed
And asked the ancient muses to unlock
The measured rhymes by which they were commanded.
I've stood where the embattled farmers stood,
My heart ablaze with pride by this soft stream
And wished that I could measure all the good
That makes us free beyond an empty dream.
But now our best-loved joys seem mottled gray,
Our expectations dulled as though we'd lost
Our bright assurance in this cloudy day
And could no longer understand the cost
    Of reinvesting in our destiny:
    O, Muse, recount again our history!

AND NOW IN PRAYER

These rugged people—this rugged land!
O, is there thanks enough to go around,
To thank them for their lives
Implanted in these Ozark Hills,
To thank this land
For metaphors it fashioned in my mind,
And to thank these people
For symbols they sculptured on my soul.

SESQUICENTENNIAL IN THE WONDER STATE

I stand alone beside an Ozark stream,
My eyes and ears attuned to every sight
And sound. I come to meditate upon
The past and to anticipate the days
And years that stretch ahead along these banks.
I'll be a witness to my own people
And land—come join me now and listen in.

To tell about these hardy pioneers,
This rugged land that calls forth rocky strength,
To write of stern landscapes and people's pain
And hardships in the days before the land
Became our much-loved state, our thanks is due
To those who persevered and left us hope,
A precious legacy to bless this day.

Some days I view an autumn sky with streaks
Of gold and crimson and a coppered sun—
The sun beholden to the maple leaves,
The sassafras and smooth-barked sycamore.
I feel the breeze that rustles each dried leaf,
I listen to the stream at Siloam Springs
That spills to winding rivers and the sea.

When winter's gone and spring enchants the air,
I stand beside a dogwood tree and feast
On blossoms one by one. Each year they come
To tell of resurrection, and I count
This day of days most treasured of the year.
Oak trees in winter, then the white dogwood,
Full-flowered—these best symbolize our land.

I think of all the leaves of yesterday,
Of all the falls and springs now come and gone
These last one-hundred-fifty years and then
Of all the fruitful lives of yesterday
And happenings in Northwest Arkansas—
The Trail of Tears that ended there in grief,
The Battle of Pea Ridge in honor fought.

Apple orchards, diamond mines, and fields
Of cotton, rice, or wheat; fat cattle on
Hill pastures where the rooster's crow is heard;
The spread of vineyards and the sweep of lakes,
The Buffalo, the Ozarks, and old mills;
Hot springs flowing, handcrafts, mountain music;
Mellow cities—all this is Arkansas,

And more! Oh, children of this gifted land,
Unite and tell the world about our love
For Arkansas, the old/young Wonder State
Where past and future seem so closely kin,
The land and people merged into a whole
As strong oaks rooted by a mountain stream
And dogwood trees that flower Easter day.

Each life, each leaf, a fragment of the whole;
This land, this people with their history
And wisdom learned from a distinctive past—
We come to celebrate our love of truth,
Our heritage of hope, and with a song
We give thanks for the poetry of life,
Learned here where tall oaks grow and dogwoods bloom.

FOREWORD TO THE FUTURE

"Enough, if something from our hands have power
To live, and act, and serve the future hour."

William Wordsworth

These pages have recorded a tradition and culture that took root and grew in the Ozark hills of Northwest Arkansas, a culture with Anglo-Saxon, Protestant origins. This is the culture I was born into, and I have sought to describe my journey in this land from childhood to old age, always conscious of its people and its culture's influence upon my life. I have wanted to express my pride and joy in this tradition, my love and feeling for the place where I belong—these hills, among these lovely people—and I have tried to relate some of my own experiences and conclusions during an important period in our history.

At the same time I have set my mind to learn about other traditions and other cultures, and to reach a synthesis in my own life. I see this as my responsibility, one small contribution to a better world.

The period I have recorded, which goes back into my grandparents' lives, roughly parallels the statehood of Arkansas, and it seems particularly appropriate that this book be published at the time when we are anticipating our sesquicentennial celebration in 1986.

Perhaps it is inevitable that a look back demands a look ahead to the next 150 years, not only for Arkansas, but for our nation and our world. None of us can continue in isolated communities with a single lifestyle. We are becoming a nation of many cultures, many societies, reflecting all the races and various creeds. Thank God for our favored country where the founders of our nation determined to provide freedom for everyone and left the Constitution whereby this freedom can be interpreted and ensured.

But I have come to realize that freedom provided by a government through its constitution is only the first step toward a better society. Freedom to be what one pleases places a responsibility upon each individual to make sure that the just laws of a free society are maintained and applied to all. The open road of freedom, when unchecked, runs wild and ends in an abyss.

The American dream for the past 150 years has been a dream of material progress, which in many ways has been realized, although there is much left to be done. And for the future? I dream of America as a leader in the world, not just in the physical sense, but in the spiritual sense—a balancing of material progress with spiritual progress.

Poetry has its place in this development. In fact, I have found poetry to be the universal factor which brings men together in an experience of the sacred dimensions of life. Poetry is neither religion nor Scripture, but it can communicate to mankind what one writer has called "the sense of participation in a timeless reality."

For my part, I met the Universal Muse, that vast and personal Love who upholds the universes and implants a sacred rhythm in all things, through the reading and writing of poetry. Because of this meeting, I now understand where the real Source of power and joy and love and life itself resides.

I dream of an America where many more will share this discovery. May the "self-reliance" taught so forcefully by Emerson translate into a new appreciation of the unique expressions of individual souls. And while individuals travel Whitman's "open road" I dream that the Universal Spirit will govern that road and guide that journey. I foresee an America where material gains take care of necessary physical needs while we press on to the spiritual riches that can give vitality and creative power to our lives.

Part II

My unconscious mind . . .
a reservoir of vast proportions,
a continent I have traveled . . .
this place where
Time has lost all dominion!

A RESERVOIR OF VAST PROPORTIONS

"Our thoughts and emotions are often but spray flung
up from hidden tides that follow a moon no eye can see. . . .
When I wrote first I wanted to describe outward things as
vividly as possible . . . and then, quite suddenly, I lost the
desire of describing outward things, and found that I took
little pleasure in a book unless it was spiritual. . . .

W. B. Yeats

Sometimes I joy to think about my unconscious mind—a
reservoir of vast proportions; a continent I have traveled every
foot of the way from babyhood to old age, from horse and buggy
travel to trips in outer space; a place filled with some successes,
many failures, and a few embarrassments I choose not to talk
about. But it is part of me. I have come to respect and appreciate
this place where time has lost all dominion and each event is
juxtaposed upon another.

I may draw an incident from out my boyhood, like plowing
with one horse in grubby land where hidden rocks and roots cause
the plow to come out of the earth and scoot along the ground—
and suddenly I live again that boyhood frustration.

Even as I am writing this, I pause to look outside my picture
window. Suddenly I see a redbird fluttering to and fro in a
dogwood tree, and the joy of nature surrounds me—its trees, its
birds, its landscape and the sky. I let this moment filter into my
unconscious mind next to the boyhood memory, and I may call
each up without regard to time. I like to think of my unconscious
mind as freed from worldly things—spirit in essence, and the
communicator between my worldly mind, my body, and the
Universal Spirit.

I have come to love and respect poetic tradition and the Scrip-
tures. I let my acceptance and the knowledge of each filter into my
unconscious where Love, Faith, and Hope heal all my inner
wounds, and thus the Universal Muse can communicate with me.
What a contrast from the view that the unconscious is a cesspool of
inhibited thoughts out of which an empty, worldly poetry grows.

Like Matthew Arnold, I still live in a wilderness and only grasp

Tom at age 6 or 7

the promised land in joyful moments—usually through poetry. I know I will continue as an ordinary, imperfect man for the remainder of my life, dwelling among failures, but as T. S. Eliot has said, my failures and the failures of my like-willed contemporaries will become the preface for success in future generations.

What a joy to be engaged in keeping alive that which is so necessary to the human spirit!

THESE WORDS WERE GATHERED

These words were gathered in the Ozark hills
Of Arkansas, like fruits and vegetables
In fall, from situations that arose
Within my years of time, accompanying
The uneven beating of this old heart—
A record of my intuitions and
Imaginations narrated and drawn
From my own memories in place and time.
I talk as though I am a prophet's voice,
But I am not; my voice may be or not.
I am a struggling ordinary man
Who chose to stand erect and listen hard.
Some days I draw my view from mountain tops,
Some days along a wooded river bank,
Some days when spring has opened up the buds,
Some days when winter winds are from the north.
As long as Time is in the stirrups, all
Conclusions are a waste of energy,
For Change is god and master of matter.
But Spirit—well, that's a different matter.

I BELONG

I belong
there is no gypsy in my blood
these hills
flow throughout my blood stream
the limestone
in my hill is magnetized
my body
is bound and imprisoned there
meanwhile
my spirit
travels throughout the universe
I belong
to all that was, that is
and is to be.

REDEMPTION

O Sacred Muse
Let me speak
In my own voice.
Let me address
The sun, the moon, and the stars
And bring
To life the inner images.
Let my words
Collect the sounds that have been true
Throughout eternity.
Dear Muse
Stand at the crossroads and direct my way
And deliver me
From the crisis of unbelief.

LEARNING THE ALPHABET

The snow began at half-past-four
And the stillness was everywhere.
The birds and all the animals
No longer moved or made a sound.

The wind joined in the quiet.
No limb or twig was moving now,
And I, observer to the fact,
Reflected on the stillness.

Each flake alone was coming down
In gentleness and silence
As though it had a single aim
To whiten all the ground as one.

This quiet caught me unaware,
But deep within I found a clue,
For stillness speaks a language too—
If one can learn the alphabet.

DECISIONS

Some days I live with all the things I know—
Four pecks make a bushel, three feet a yard,
Water moving by a gravity flow,
And poems written by a mundane bard.
These days I travel on well-beaten roads,
Highway Five-Forty or One-Twenty-One.
I observe all the traditional codes
And sing with friends and neighbors in unison.
On other days I deal with mystic things,
The new, and travel with the avant-garde
To strange and mysterious happenings,
Through unknown lands without a bodyguard,
To travel on a rugged thoroughfare
Where grave decisions greet me everywhere.

YOUR SONGS IN ME

O Sacred Muse, come be my honored guest
And heal the conflict in my troubled soul.
Direct me on this mundane earthbound quest
With holy images that make me whole.
O Sacred Muse, I feel your presence now,
Each metered rhyme resounding deep in me;
I find your peaceful message can endow
Old age and restless youth with harmony.
O Sacred Muse, I thank you for your care,
And now my life is metered by your rhyme;
I own the honor and the joy to share
Your everlasting Love in my own time.
    Your songs in me have made my life anew;
    With grateful heart I sing in praise of you.

AN OPTIMIST'S VIEW OF NATURALISM

> "Naturalism is the aesthetic correlate of a philososphical doctrine that has its place in 19th-c. history. It is a movement, and not merely a way of looking at things. . . . The writer (is urged) to imitate the scientist by observing reality (the *how*) without inquiring into its ultimate causes (the *why*)."
>
> *Princeton Encyclopedia of Poetry and Poetics*

Naturalism as a word has a nice ring to it. It makes one think of a cozy log fire crackling in a mountain cabin, or fresh vegetables on the table, or a young girl who looks wholesome and charming without cosmetics.

But naturalism means something quite different! According to the *Random House Dictionary,* naturalism is a view of the world which takes account only of natural elements and forces, excluding the supernatural or spiritual. It is the belief that all phenomena are covered by laws of science and that all teleological explanations are without value. Teleological explanations refer to the goals and purposes behind what we see. In other words, naturalism believes that the existence of our universe and all that happens within it is *without* purpose and meaning!

Tragically, this outlook is the worldview predominantly held in the last half of the twentieth century, a view nurtured as doctrinal truth by our secular world. Such a view must foster pessimism, for it means that our world has no hope beyond the material benefits that science *may* be able to provide *if* we manage to survive such scientific advances as germ warfare and nuclear fission.

But I am an optimist who believes that this obsession with science and materialism is a phase which will be replaced in the next century by a searching for what I call First Things. Even today, men are surely more than secular. They are more than utilitarian.

As Louis MacNeice has observed, "Life—let alone art— cannot be assessed purely in terms of utility. Food, for example, is useful for life but what is life useful for?. . . . The faith in the value of living is a mystical faith. The pleasure in bathing or dancing, in colour or shape, is a mystical experience. It is because I do not think of men as essentially utilitarian that I maintain that poetry is a normal activity, that the poet is a specialist in something which everyone practices."

To discover poetry in nature is a mystical experience, because the tall oak tree, the dogwood bloom, the mountain stream, speak of the power that rules the universe and maintains the forces of life in order and continuity.

A. W. Tozer has described the Christian mystic in this way: "The mystic . . . experiences his faith down in the depths of his sentient being. . . . He exists in a world of spiritual reality. He is quietly, deeply, and sometimes almost ecstatically aware of the Presence of God in his own nature and in the world around him. His religious experience is something elemental, as old as time and the creation. It is immediate acquaintance with God by union with the Eternal Son. It is to know that which passes knowledge."

In contrast, a belief in naturalism gives man the false impression that *he* is god and controller of nature—a belief that leads to chaos and oblivion.

Of course, dictators and tyrannical systems of government prefer the doctrine of naturalism. It keeps people in bondage without hope—helpless, with nothing beyond themselves. But dictators can never stamp out the individual spirit of men and women who embrace the First Things of Love, Faith, and Hope, and in the process find the meaning of their life.

I can afford to be an optimist because I inhabit "a world of spiritual reality."

BEYOND ALL TIMES

I've been at the borning of time—
Crocus peeping out of the ground,
Solitary and showy,
To tell that spring is here again.

I've been at the bounty of time—
The fruits of life in abundance,
All things alive and growing,
Provided for by the sun and rain.

I've been at the zenith of time—
With fruits and vegetables in store,
Magnificent colors, and grand
In autumn's sunset glow.

I've been at the dying of time—
Ushered in by cold northern winds,
The grass and leaves buried deep
Beneath the sleet and ice and snow.

I've been at time beyond time—
And listened to an inner voice.
I've found there's more to gain with Love
Than power, prestige, or yellow gold.

DISCOVERY

I have labored
With the contrariety of tones,
Of hawk and mockingbird.
I have listened
To Einstein, Wordsworth, and Emerson,
To the mystery of things and to reality.
I have been alone
As on an island surrounded by the sea,
Myself the only inhabitant.
I have been in the market place,
A single person, surrounded
By the babble of voices everywhere.
I have measured my own self
And found it valuable and unique.
I have traveled an open road
Without rule or regulation and have foreseen
Its tragic end.
At last I have discovered
A synthesis
Where Love encompasses all.

64

EACH SEASON IS A SONNET

I've watched the seasons come and go each year
And searched and found a song in every one;
A joyful song inside this sonneteer
To greet each time and pray for unison.
In spring and summertime I praise the growth
Of life and plants and every living thing;
In fall and wintertime I measure both
For all the joy of harvest they can bring.
Each season is a sonnet written bold
In nature's time and place—a hidden call,
An inner song for man to find and hold,
The stressed and unstressed merged into the all.
    A life is but four seasons tied to Time
    In which to learn about eternal rhyme.

CONTINUITY

Beneath
a stationary blue sky
white cumulus clouds
composed of restless atoms
constantly changing form
move steadily eastward
above
my Ozark home in springtime.

Two robins
outside my picture window
have chosen a nesting place
foretelling speckled eggs,
hungry mouths, and fledgling wings.

Summer,
autumn and cold north winds,
a journey south,
and dreams of spring again.

DRY SEASONS

Among these hills
I've witnessed
The seasons come and go.
Each one
Has special things to say
To me,
The frost, the ice, the sleet and snow,
The wind, the heat and cold, the rain.

Then a word or phrase
Will come, pure and unthought,
And I am taught
As in a class in school
That there are gardens
Deep within myself
I need to cultivate,
And in dry seasons
To carry water to the wilted plants.

THE TURN AROUND

The days
come and go.

Some
are handsomer than others.
Some
are ragged, heartsick and sore,
and that's the way it is today.

It's autumn
and there are no apples on my trees.
A freeze last spring
killed all the blossoms
that would be apples now.

But never mind,
I'm going to turn this day around
and tell the world
that I control my own weather!

Twelve months from now
I may be picking apples
on a handsome day
because I turned this time around.

REFLECTING IN DECEMBER'S SUN

The old year ends
splashed
in a late December sun,
and silently
another ring has formed
around each and every tree.

While reflecting on the matter
I envisioned
all the valleys and the hills
encompassed into one
and now I know
more than the years
are being recorded
in the rings around my body.

IMPEDIMENTS NO LONGER ARE

Sometimes
my old house seems cobwebby
and dusty.

Outside
the wilderness seems to be taking over.
Broad paths that once went everywhere
are grown up with blackberry vines,
with barbs that pierce and draw blood,
that keep me from venturing out
and hold me here in this old house
where eerie sounds are heard.

My spirit comes and counsels me.

I grab a broom
and sweep the dust from this old house.
I brush the cobwebs from my beams.
I clear
the brambles from my path.

And what used to be impediments no longer are.

GROWING

These streams, these trees, these valleys—
Youth, middle age, and old age,
And I have reckoned with them all.
The wind, the rain, the sleet and snow
Have come and left me sad and wounded.
But spring has come and all is well again.
I know that dusty winds and rocky roads
Are bound to be my host.
But who am I to curse this providence?
Out of growing older my spirit grows.
Oh, tall oak trees, the handsomest of all
Beside the streams and in the valleys,
Through years of wind, of rain, of sleet and snow,
How many redbirds have nestled within your boughs?

THE GREATER CHALLENGES

Challenges
accept a call
from somewhere deep within.
The greater ones are long term:
they begin in youth,
take deep root,
grow and expand in middle years.
In old age they touch the sky.

EIGHTY-TWO AND CLIMBING

The air is turning somewhat rare.
My body hates the change in temperature.
My breath comes in uneven spells.
My eyes have blurred the landscape
And my ears have muffled its sounds.
My spirit scoffs at all this failing stuff
And tells my body to relax
For all physical journeys are due to end.
My spirit's been a good and faithful companion
Over a long and rugged road,
And—now my body's eighty-two and failing—
My spirit's up and climbing.

ETERNAL SPRINGS

Hope is a morning and an evening star
That shines on me in darkness and the light;
It cancels needless dread, alarm, and fright
And rides on wheels without a single jar.
It takes my hand and leads me near and far,
I feel its presence in the darkest night,
I recognize its skills with pure delight
And with its help I cross each rocky bar.
Hope springs eternal in the human breast,
The poets tell us in a thousand ways,
And I have reason to believe their word,
For by hope's aid I often have been blest.
With joy it comes to freshen up my days,
And greets the dawn much like a singing bird.

EDITORIAL COMMENT

This old manuscript
Has eighty-two chapters written
In four sections—
A spring, a summer, an autumn, and winter.
My editor keeps guiding me
To new and interesting experiences.
Just yesterday
Intuition took me far beyond this land
To link me with thoughts eternal.
Although
My local vision seems to dim
This other vision gleams brighter every day.
Some days
I reconstruct my past
And blend it with present and future
In search of the whole.
I have no idea
How many chapters are left
In this old manuscript
But I am going to keep on writing
As though there were no end to them
And when the last one has been written,
As it is sure to be,
I hope the publishers will add this epitaph:

"The author had a feeling
  On life, on death,
  That they were only
  The preface to eternity."

CERTAINTY

One Sunday morning at half past eight
On my way to view the universe
I entered through a wooded lane
And passed by dogwood trees in bloom.

I stooped beside a spring-fed stream
And heard it murmuring among the rocks.
The limestone ledge above it
Spelled out solidity,
While all around I found uncertainties
Where floods had come and caused the dirt to move,
And in a sudden rush the rocks and pebbles too.

Then silently
I stood beneath a white oak tree
And listened . . .
I seemed to hear a strain of music
Not far away.

If this is what the Universe is like
I have no death to fear.

LISTENING

I have stood and listened
To the Pacific Ocean beat
Against a California shore
And watched the water settle back
Into the sea amidst the presence of its own white foam.
On a balmy day
I have watched the Atlantic Ocean gently roll
Against a sandy shore,
The beach receiving and rejecting the water's even flow.
I have stood high in the atmosphere
On a Colorado mountain peak
And visioned
Miles and miles of landscape.
I have waited in heavy woods
And listened to a distant waterfall.
I have stood on the border
Between the United States and Canada
And watched thousands of tons of water
Fall into the caverns below.
But there is more to nature
Than its water and its foam,
Its mountain peaks, its rugged jagged shores,
Or its smooth sandy beaches, or its waterfalls:
There is grandeur in the landscape and the sky.
I have seen it in a rainbow,
In a summer sunrise or an autumn sunset,
Or a full moon in the east.
I have seen and heard all nature murmuring
In a rapid mountain stream,
And I have grasped
The wholeness of the Universe in one dogwood bloom.

THE UNRECORDED HEIGHTS

I view the colors in an autumn sun—
No night or death in winter's waiting call,
Only the joy that spring and summer won—
And feel that I am master of it all.
New worlds explode across my western sky:
My autumn sun has brought in view new sights,
Each one a wonder to my inner eye
Where I can view the unrecorded heights.
My Muse has joined a universal band
Where thought and feeling speak a common tongue,
Where rhymes and meters dance to her command
And at her call the finest songs are sung.
    This joy my faith has opened up to me
    To celebrate and share through poetry.

THE GIFT

I

It's springtime
In the Ozark hills of Arkansas
On Easter Sunday
With dogwood trees in bloom.

I stand beside a tall oak tree
And entertain a silent prayer.

Immediately
I feel the rush of inner potencies
Within a cold and heartless earth
To push through the surfaces
And be born again.

I feel the cruel pangs of birth
Yet I enter into the joy and laughter
Afterward.

Without the pain
How could the joy and laughter form?

II

I ask a simple question.
Where does the Love come from
To cause the dogwood tree to bloom,
To cause the oak and maple trees
To bud and spread their leaves,
To cause the sun to rise and spend
Its energy to make them grow,
To cause the rain to fall and nourish everything,
To cause the eyes and ears within this simple one
To make a record of these things and ask in prayer,
Where does the Love come from?

III

Now it's summer
And matter seems to be
The object of the universe,
For many have labored long and hard
Without the prayer
And did build for themselves
Earthly mansions on this earth
To live splendidly in a consumer's paradise.
Mission accomplished:
Life without immortality,
Spirit atropied like a withered hand,
The self supreme,
No other worlds to conquer,
All that's left,
To live and die like any animal.

IV

Autumn's breath is in the air.
A lizard stops
Then runs along an old rail fence.
A wasp
Moves slowly
Drugged by the cold north wind.

A cricket
Lies dead, upturned upon the ground.
The leaves
Of maple, dogwood and sassafras
Are yellow, brown and red,
Though oak leaves
Gleam green as ever.
An occasional one
Has turned bright yellow,
And I stand here
An observer to dying things,
My body carefully reading the signs.
Yet I am comforted.
My spirit awaits its tryst
With destiny.

V

The birds are gone
And summer's goods like the reptiles
Lie harbored in the ground,
The ice and snow in charge of everything.
I have lived and reckoned
With the seasons,
With birth and death
And found them great and full of meaning,
Yet insignificant.
For I make connection
With a rhythm deep within.

VI

It comes
Like a flash of lightning
On my mind
And every atom in my body
Glows and trembles with joy
As I view
Bare limbs outlined
Against the sky.

In one short second
All the universe
Opens up to me
And I am free
To choose my words
And tell
What I have seen.

VII

It comes as a gift
From somewhere deep within.
It closes
As it opened up.
Yet
In this moment of excitement
All my bound and unbound energies are one.
What a joy
To know the Sacred Muse is a continuum
And with each meeting
My life is made anew!

FAITH AND IMAGINATION

"Behold, the kingdom of God is within you."

Luke 17:21

The question is often asked: Is there any relationship between religion and poetry? Of course, the secular world gives a resounding "No!"

I would like to rephrase the question and make it specific rather than general, directing it to individuals: Do you feel there is a relationship between your faith and your imagination?

My answer, of course, would be, "Yes, poetic faith and poetic imagination *are* related." This immediately puts me in a different category from the ranks of many well-known and widely acclaimed poets. It is evident that the way each one answers this question will determine the type of poetry that is produced.

In my position, I write poetry out of a feeling of security in two worlds, one of the body and one of the spirit. In the body I live in the physical world, and in my spirit, I live in the spiritual world. My faith becomes the connecting link between the two worlds, and my imagination is the vehicle by which transition is made.

I find it joy to call upon my imagination to exercise its powers in both worlds, for to let the power of imagination be exercised in one world only is to live an incomplete life. Thus, I write poetry expressed in concrete terms, and I write poetry expressed in the language of the spirit, using abstract words that represent warm and wonderful Reality.

To recognize the reality of two worlds is to take nothing away from the scientist with his preoccupation with the physical world and his growing knowledge of it. But imagination without faith makes man a loner, adrift in one world, and leaves him to explore his own imagination without any guidance or restrictions, without love for his fellow man, his destination an abyss of chaos.

Czeslaw Milosz in *The Witness of Poetry* describes the "totally objective, cold, indifferent world from which the Divine Imagination has been alienated," and the rapid erosion of belief in any world other than one submitted to a mathematical determinism.

Tom at his typewriter

In contrast, faith and love linked to the imagination create a very different kind of effect. The imagination is the author of our literature, good or bad. When we recognize the relationship of personal faith and the imagination, then we realize the responsibility that lies upon all writers, indeed, upon all artists who work with the imagination. Will our work have value? The answer may depend upon the question posed at the first: Is there a relationship between your faith and your imagination?

Part III

In an age of prose,
why write poetry?

I write
because
to be a part
of this endless communion
is the greatest thing
that has happened
to me
in a long and happy life.

POETRY: AN ENDLESS COMMUNION

"I would have related, had I known how, everything which
a single memory can gather for the praise of men.
O sun, o stars, I was saying, holy, holy, holy, is our being
beneath heaven and the day and our endless communion."

Czeslaw Milosz

In an age of prose, why write poetry? It's an honest question
which I am often asked. Poetry has ceased to be a natural and
necessary commodity in our day. With so little demand for it, why
write it at all? Each poet has a different answer, and here is mine.

Poetry came to me late in life after fifty years devoted to
banking, my family, and my community. Now, eleven years into
retirement, I am deeply devoted to my new work, that of poetry.

These years have been so enjoyable, and no small part of that is
due to the host of new friends I have found in poetry. I can almost
say that I didn't discover poetry; that poetry discovered me. It has
delivered me from a life of despair in a rocking chair and has
provided a whole new universe out there for me to explore.

If I were to attempt to define poetry, I would say that it deals
with first things, with universal things, with the absolute, the
world in unity, while prose deals with particulars, the relative, the
concrete, a world in conflict. Each individual must find a synthesis
in his own life, balancing these two worlds so that somehow a
unity evolves. In my case, the synthesis I discovered is not new, but
the old, old synthesis of Love, Faith, and Hope.

My experiences have taught me that happiness springs out of a
life committed in both the physical and spiritual worlds, and I
recognize a need for acceptance of both authority and tradition. I
know that each person on this planet is important and unique, but
individuals must fit their own uniqueness into the authority and
tradition of the universe.

I accept the Spiritual Universe as the governing body of all
matter, and its Universal Muse (an unfamiliar term in this secular
age) is within the grasp of every person through the individual's
imagination. As I continue to journey in my physical body, these
moments of the spiritual journey that burst suddenly upon my

consciousness are the greatest moments of my life. These moments we joyfully call poetry, although many hours of work and revision may be required before the poem fits properly into the creative life of the universe.

T. S. Eliot suggested that the poet in any age needs to express with individual differences the general state of mind; that by writing himself, he writes his time. In writing myself and my time, I am intensely aware of the rich, meaningful tradition of poetry that has the ring of truth, from Dante through Matthew Arnold through Eliot and onward, always active, always continuing. I suggest that it is the plain duty of poets to reiterate from time to time that genuine poetry is conceived in the soul and spirit, not composed by the wits of man!

I write poetry because to be a part of this endless communion is the greatest thing that has happened to me in a long and happy life.

THE POETIC
STRAIN

In these United States of America
At home on top an Ozark hill
I reach for pen and yellow pad.
I feel the urge to write, confident
The poetic strain will summon me
Throughout the Universe
And link
My self and soul with poets everywhere—
A faith
Long harbored deep within myself.

I view the little creek below,
The trees, the landscape and the sky.
I let my mind encompass time,
Two thousand years and more into the past.
I love my country and its laws,
The people and the land,
Yet I am mindful of its evil days,
The Trail of Tears and slavery,
And injustices that need correcting.
While I am grieved
By the conflict, wars and violence
Everywhere upon the planet,
I seek and hope and pray
For better times
Before the year Two-Thousand comes.

I search for words
To wed the rural and urban lands,
And rhyme the landscape with the factory.
I think of language and its mighty role
Which leads
The human race to greater heights
Or else
To broaden more their fallen state.
As I look to literature to find the answer
To the mystery of life, then

As in a flash, I see the truth:
The self and soul are one in poetry.
And with this theme in mind I feel an inner urge
That forward from this day I will renew
My faith in God and tell about
His reign of Love and Truth in poetry.

I will redo
My worldly aims and balance mind and soul.
I'll use the sun instead of fossil oil
Where possible
And make all nature pure again,
And sing my praise in poetry.
I'll write about the wholeness of the Universe
To bridge the gap that has been formed
And link the self and soul, and praise all nature too.
I welcome doors that open up my mind
To nature's creativity.
I stand in awe before a dogwood tree in spring.
Its blossoms,
Red or white or pink,
Impress themselves upon my soul
And cause my mind
To gather words and thoughts
I never knew before.

Oh, what a joy to speak these words
And know
I too can blossom in the spring!
I stand beneath
A tall oak tree in my backyard
And wonder
At its grace and symmetry.
I think of it
As nature's greatest specimen.
Throughout these years
It's been my constant guide,
It's taught me how to look for dappled things,
For spots that added pleasure to my life,
To recognize the many joys that nature holds

And tell of them so everyone may share.
All nature writes a sacred song
Beyond the reach of local time and space.
An acorn grows into a tall oak tree,
Its continuity an inner rhyme.

I write this praise
To nature with great joy
Where spots in time
Have caused my soul to grow.
And now I write
A praise to poets everywhere
No matter what the faith, the tribe, or dialect.
Let us recognize our common ground,
Regardless of our individualities,
And though our souls must differ,
They combine to make
The wholeness of the Universe complete.
Open the locks to cheerfulness and sing:
For too long now
Our themes have been diversity,
An open road each took by himself
That ended in a darkened wood.
Now let us be true to God, to family, and friends,
And let our character and our will
Be molded by the Universal Muse.

ALMOST ANYTHING BUT THE TRUTH

" 'Nowadays' is a civilization in which the prime emblems of poetry are dishonored. In which serpent, lion and eagle belong to the circus-tent; ox, salmon and boar to the cannery; race-horse and grey-hound to the betting ring; and the sacred grove to the saw-mill. In which the Moon is despised as a burned-out satellite of the Earth and woman reckoned as 'auxiliary State personnel.' In which money will buy almost anything but the truth, and almost anyone but the truth-possessed poet."

Robert Graves

Much modern poetry, it seems, is little more than something that will make do, that "will suffice" like the passing excitement of a football game or a sexual fling, something for the hour because only the present is important; the past, the future, to be blotted out. No motto worth writing to hang on the wall. Former texts are broken vessels to be swept up and hauled away with the garbage, while the poets of the day concentrate on the bizarre, the brilliant, the momentarily thrilling.

But do not let us be downhearted; let us assume that present poetry is in a temporary phase that will be overcome, that a new day has already begun for many poets of this generation.

In the twenties Wallace Stevens led the revolt against "religious presuppositions" and chose to present the death of the old gods as a "liberation of the imagination." Our paradise is within this world, he claimed. Poets can actually replace religious beliefs with their own verse, he believed.

Today, this arrogance of seeing in oneself the power to replace the Creator in the hungers of man's soul seems truly remarkable. Poets are only men, after all, who need to remember the true source of power as they work. I predict that a generation of poets is coming who will return to the great poetry of the past to produce a work in harmony with all that has met the test of time; that the continuity of traditional poetry will be maintained with a renewal of vision; that new mottoes will be written worth hanging upon our walls!

BRIDGES AND BUILDING BLOCKS

To bridge the gap
from man to man
first
let me heal
the conflict in myself
then
let me work
with building blocks
to speak an ordered conversation,
thought and feeling interacting,
argument making rhythm
when words declare the truth.

IN THE SPIRIT OF SOCRATES

I was born on the sixth day of May
Four hundred sixty years
Before the time of Christ.

My wants were few and modest
For I knew the simple life was best.
I felt a guiding principle within
More valuable than any outside source.
With my intellect and feeling in harmony
A special kind of joy prevailed
In my every wish and will.
It was as if my soul
Were speaking to my self,
Telling it to be humble,
Yet assertive,
With force and energy
To seek the greater things of life,
But under no circumstance
To let my self resort to sentimentality
Or destructive criticism.

I thank the spirit's presence
Deep within myself
That spoke to me so early in my life
About the love of wisdom.
This caused me to wonder
Why man spends so little time
Seeking to overcome his ignorance.
I always counted it a shame
To drift into old age
Without improving to the utmost
Those faculties
Nature has given free.

To practice what I preached
I learned to play the lyre,
To write some poetry,
And put Aesop's Fables in verse
In my old age.

So let my poetic statement be
To everyone everywhere:
"Expel the ignorance and know thyself."

FOR ARCHIBALD MacLEISH 1892-1982

You were born in Glencoe, Illinois,
Before this century began;
You died a citizen of all the land.
Your life was acted out
In the public eye of the Twentieth Century
As lawyer, poet, librarian, bureaucrat, journalist,
Diplomat, publicist, professor, and critic.
You were social and unalienated,
Affectionate, generous, and happy—
Like all of us, at times fearful, vain, and thin-skinned.
You had your score of friends and enemies too.
You were accepted in the highest circles,
But not in some you thought you should have been.
Some said you were an imitator,
Knowledgeable in the technicalities,
And not the greatest poet,
But you knew as we all know
That reviews are written
In the subjective mood.

Convictions grew in you
Like corn
In well-fertilized and cultivated land
To furnish nourishment and sustenance
For many.

Yale and your mother
Nurtured you into evangelical inclinations
And made you what some have called
A secular priest.

Like a masculine line ending in poetry,
There was no falling off of energy in you;
Each and every syllable
In your life was stressed.
You were a poet and a public man.
Although, in your ending,

There was a quietness,
A softness of feeling,
And a lingering of thought
That will remain in American poetry
To mold the parts into a whole
That will forever Be.

UNIVERSAL TALK

One day in April
I sat
beneath a tall oak tree
on top
an Ozark hill in Arkansas
and viewed
the resurrection everywhere.
I saw a dogwood tree in bloom,
the reddened buds of maple trees,
the tender leaves of sassafras and oak,
with songbirds for my orchestra.

Suddenly
?y imagination was roaming
throughout the universe
and ancient poets were in my company.

Dante
and an American Indian poet
and I
discussed the nature of the universe
and found
more good than bad to talk about.

NO LONGER ALONE WITH AMERICA

> "I am not a Russian poet and it's always astonishing for
> me to be taken for one. One becomes a poet not to be
> French, Russian, etc., but to be everything. More exactly:
> one is a poet because one is *not* French. . . . Orpheus
> explodes one's nationality, or enlarges it to such a point that
> everyone (present and past) is included within it . . . "

Marina Tsvetayeva in a letter to Rilke

There is a wildness and freedom in American literature that I
love, especially as characterized by Walt Whitman's "Open
Road" and Emerson's "Self-Reliance," but I acknowledge that
with some serious reservations.

In 1984 American poetry is traveling an unrestricted road that
I cannot follow. Through Ezra Pound's "the image is the symbol,"
Carlos William's "No idea but in things," and Wallace Stevens'
"the supreme fiction," American poetry has become almost
totally secular.

For my part, faith in the Love that rules the universes is the
indispensable factor which provides the road signs on my open
road, which saves me from destruction, which protects me from an
inordinate self-reliance and self-preoccupation, and that keeps me
from ending up in an abyss such as Stevens describes: *"palm at the
end of mind—on the edge of space."*

I am no longer "alone with America." I belong to all the world
and to poetry of universal scope reflecting unchanging truth. I
believe it is time for America to put her poetry back on track and
join the ranks of poets of universal significance. In short, I
am saying that Emerson and Whitman offer an incomplete
philosophy apart from the balancing contributions of Dante and
other wise poets of the ages. Nationality is of no significance.

Of course, I am proud to be called an American, and I
recognize that Emerson, Whitman, Williams, and Stevens have
contributed an appreciation of the individual's importance which
is valuable indeed. I have received helpful insights through their
poetry, and I have found my imagination opening up under their
prodding. But they have been seen as *more* than they are, as

purveyors of truth, rather than struggling poets caught within their own conflicts. As a result, many have accepted their conclusions as valid, and have moved along the road that will lead to the abyss.

As an optimist, I look forward to the time when our poets will no longer be "alone with America," but will write universal poetry that reflects the needs and aspirations and spiritual hungers of all men.

FREE TO TRAVEL

This morning
I sit at my desk—
Homer, Virgil, Dante, Chaucer, Shakespeare
And all the modern poets at my fingertips
in a thousand books or more,
arranged haphazardly in shelves on my wall.

I am an American citizen
born to all its rights and privileges.

At times my mind will catch a line or two
from the Odyssey,
then maybe from Eliot, Wordsworth, or Wallace Stevens.

Soothingly, I'll hear
a whippoorwill, a mockingbird, a meadowlark.

Then, distractingly, I'll hear
a coyote howl, a vicious tiger or a lion roar.

But, happily,
my mind's worn calluses (as on my hands)
from lifting burdens almost too heavy to bear.

Now
I am free to travel
throughout this rugged Universe.

NEW SCENERY

My Muse is like a sea-bound albatross
With skill to stay aloft long lengths of time;
Each soaring flight into the new, across
Untraveled seas to scenes of the sublime.
Each scene a star as though it were my own
And ever-present, waiting to be found;
A world that's full of places to be known
Where man and albatross are kindred bound.
Yet poetry is man's most noble task
In search of broader visions in the mind,
With new and untold visions to unmask
And open up new worlds for all mankind.
 And now I wait to view new scenery
 And lend my love and voice to poetry.

MOLDING OF THE OPPOSITES

Some days I've been a fundamentalist,
Some days I've been a liberal,
Some days I'm very conservative,
Some days I'm all for progress and reform.
But now that I have found myself in poetry
Its metaphor and symbol have taught me many things.

I look upon my days of conflict with chagrin,
And recognize the dialectical process as real
And active in all matter's world.
But spirit is a different matter
And speaks a different language.
While science is the language of matter
And is always searching for truth in its own world,
I've found that poetry can speak the language of another world.
And neither can be reckoned by the other.

I've studied Blake and Yeats
And the interacting of the opposites.
What a joy
To know they can be harmonized
With Love, and Faith, and Hope.

WITH ROBERT FROST IN THE SHADOWS

It's mid-January
And no snow has fallen.
The limbs of trees are bare,
Outstretched against the sky.
Suddenly, two cardinals
Take possession of a dogwood tree
Directly in front of my picture window.
Then a dozen blackbirds or maybe more
Come flying into my view
From out of nowhere.
A little later, two squirrels
Seem to have urgent business on my lawn.
All this is happening on my hillside
In full view of a spring-fed stream
Meandering through the little valley below,
While a gentle wind is moving fallen leaves
Across dry grass.

It's suppertime now and my wife Grayce
And I live dangerously tonight—
Fresh strawberries, German chocolate cake
And a dish of ice cream.

The news at six
Reports the prime rate went down
And the stock market went up 50 points
To the highest ever.

Then we settle down
To hear the MacNeil-Lehrer Report—
An in-depth treatment of some current problem.

But I am becoming restless,
For deep inside, somewhere,
A gentle wind is moving me
And I have images to make
And metaphors to draw
Before I sleep.

BEYOND THE SEEN

I've seen the sunrise in an Ozark stream
And heard the water sing among the rocks:
A song that's real as in a perfect scheme
Where all the codes are pure and orthodox.
I've seen the sunset in an autumn sky,
The mighty sun so big, so red, so round,
And listened to the landscapes testify,
My self attuned to every sight and sound.
Yet nature brings but partial joy unless
Its artistry is linked beyond the seen
And heard, to cause the spirit to express
A joy where conflict cannot intervene.
    And when I feel these inner joys unfold
    I search for words to share what can be told.

AFFIRMATIONS

I write about a joy that has been known
In every form of art and poetry,
About the sudden joy an artist feels
When intuitions mothered deep within
Begin to form upon his consciousness—
The moment of all moments in his life,
A joy full term and ready to be born.
How does he know his images are true
And not wild specters from a lawless sea
Emerging from an inner formlessness?
His only clue, an inborn urge to be
Himself and build his own identity
As honored member of the Universe.
The artist, long a seeker of the truth
Within his own creative mind, has found
A joyful freedom in his art and lets
It happen as it may, in answer to
His individual view. He then can know
The old, the very old held deep within,
Will blossom in due time with splendid shoots.

AS SEEDS IN NATURE

A poet has said
That "the passionate love of words"
Is a prerequisite for writing poetry
And I would not disagree.
But there is more, much more.
For words
Like seeds in nature
Are one's own thoughts and imaginings
Germinating in fertile beds,
Drawing substances
From the inner regions of the soul,
Shaped
To become a poem
Full-grown,
Its roots
Extending deep into the past,
Its limbs
Reaching high into the future.

A POET'S DESTINY

The sacred rhythms of the Universe
Were there before the origin of man;
Now they reside within the poet's verse
According to the Universal Plan.
Each poet has a gifted need to write
And speak in his or her own voice;
The rhythms come much like a meteorite
To cause the mind to sparkle and rejoice.
True poetry, a noble work of art
That chooses words and syllables in rhyme,
Must meter them upon the poet's heart
In themes connected to eternal time.
    So bid to find a poet's destiny
    Where self and soul are one in harmony.

DISCIPLINE

> "It is the task of poetry to ensure the survival of traditional bonds of 'civitas' that exist   among people organically—and make up man's rootedness . . . Even if we leave no immortal works behind us, the discipline itself is worthy of praise."

Czeslaw Milosz

Poets and critics of poetry have generally overlooked, or completely rejected, one of the most important factors in writing poetry, and that factor is discipline. As Milosz has said, the importance does not lie in writing immortal poetry—immortal poets are few and far between!— but what it does in the life of the poet and the example offered to his time and his place.

Thus, a poetry of disciplined optimism is poetry worthy of praise, not so much for what the poet says, but because of the life and energy back of the poem. In the past several decades, of course, the poem has received all the attention of the critics, and what the poet stood for counted for nothing. Ironically, many times the poet with the least discipline in his life received the greatest acclaim. Even now, the new critics talk only about the text, and the individual poet is of little significance.

Some valuable poetry has been written in this harsh age out of great suffering, pain, and the enslaving of millions of people. As Leon Wieseltier has observed, "This is the century for which the spiritual should be the most obvious. How could the slaughters of Hitler and Stalin, and the Communist captivity of half of Europe and most of Asia, not shake the soul?"

Other poets nurtured in the ease and freedom of America own the opportunity, the duty, the responsibility and—even more— the delight of disciplining themselves to write their own individual, unique poetry out of a disciplined and unified spirit and body, and through their lives as poets to contribute to the welfare of humankind.

THE POETRY DOES MATTER

Sometimes I leave computers filled with facts
And seek a rendezvous with poetry.
I find a joy, so fresh, so frank, so true,
I keep a record of it in a poem,
For intuition has a way with words
That science cannot state in formula.
I try new ways to let my joy be known,
For words get worn out like a suit of clothes
And metaphors need freshening up a bit.
Now I have found the still point in this world
That joins up with an everlasting sphere.
I joy to enter in this sacred place
And read inscriptions on some timeless wall
Where all the words are writ in capitals.

SOME THOUGHTS ON POETRY

The joys of poetry shouldn't be hidden
Like needles in the hay.
Symbols should be warm-hearted and living
And not like water frozen into icicles.
The themes already have been written
And spoken in sacred script to man.
All myth and myth-making should be eliminated.
The sacred muse speaking to the unique poet
Should be all the newness that is needed.

POETRY IS MORE THAN ...

Confound it, Auden!
Poetry does make things happen.
Ezra Pound, you old rascal!
Not everything can be made concrete and new.
Walt Whitman, contain yourself!
An open road without authority leads to an abyss.
Wallace Stevens, you should have learned to love!
Poetry is more than a fiction
Created in your imagination.

To all you lovers of particulars,
From now on, my poetry will be whole.
I'll tell of Love and Faith and Hope
Engendered deep beyond all local time and space.
Sometimes I'll bring my writing down to earth
In concrete things wonderful and real.
But I'll be seeking all the while
To link my life and yours with Universal Love.

THE UNSEEN POTENCY

All words are full of energy. I've heard
A poet say "This must suffice me here"
And another "to find what will suffice"—
The words somehow assembled in their minds
To say what they believed belonged to them
And in their mind invent a universe.
To see the words in action in my life
Or know them as a symbol in my verse
Tells me the world is not my own idea.
Back there somewhere a power base exists
That caused chaos to change to ordered form.
I can call upon this transcendent force
· And feel its Universal form in me,
But if I misappropriate the words
I hear but echoes of my emptiness.

WORDS AND ATOMS

Like atoms
forming a tree
on planet earth

Or galaxies
in the great expanse
of space

Words assemble
in the poet's
mind.

Like atoms
they hold
untold energy

Their splitting
an ordained
freedom.

Poets, each
uniquely endowed,
must decide

To engage in dialectics
or fuse into
the unity of Love.

For individuals
created like
any tree or galaxy

Own an overpowering
exception: a spirit
within to choose

Life with the Creator
or death with all the trees
and old galaxies.

POETRY REVIEW IN THE SAHARA

All poetry without deep-rooted love
Is lonely sand found in a desert place,
With empty words expressing hopeless themes
In arid verse without the gift of grace.

SUNDAY MORNING

" . . . they be blind leaders of the blind. And if the blind
lead the blind, both shall fall into the ditch."

Matthew 15:14

Schopenhauer ("The world is my idea") and Nietzsche ("God
is dead") as well as Einstein and Freud must have been much on
the mind of Wallace Stevens when he wrote "Sunday Morning."
Some have said that this poem is a hymn of humanism where all is
relative. They agree with him that there is no absolute, that "we
live in an old chaos of the sun." They too believe that the physical
universe is the only one; there is no spiritual universe, and like a
casual flock of pigeons we are all destined to sink downward to
darkness on extended wings, without meaning, without human
feeling.

Jesus in this poem is seen as merely another poet, a humanist
like Stevens, whose poetry is fiction growing out of the imagina-
tion; that because "death is the mother of beauty," his death is like
that of any other man whose beauty is born of death.

The time is overdue for poets to begin evaluating this
turbulent century, especially those of us whose experiences date
back to its very beginning. We need to put that experience on
record for other generations. It has been a traumatic experience
with strange new theories in philosophy, psychology, and science.
It has meant the destruction of old beliefs and traditions, and, in
the way that poets shape an age, Wallace Stevens has been a key
figure in these destructions.

In his "The Man with the Blue Guitar," for example, he seems
to represent a dialog with life in the twentieth century growing out
of these very difficult times, but his poetry is tragic and ends in an
abyss.

In an interesting way, my personal dialog with him has helped
me resolve my own problems of faith. Through understanding his
order of poetry, I have been better able to establish my own and to
express my faith under the new and difficult knowledge that has
come into our lives.

This book is a channel for the expression of my faith in these experiences and my joy in the resolution of faith—a resolution that unites the new theories of matter where knowledge is paramount with the old theory, older than the hills, of faith operating in man's spirit where the intuition and discernment of the spirit are paramount. As Dante saw it: "Instinct and intellect balanced equally . . ."

Listen to the wild beauty of Stevens' "Sunday Morning": *"Complacencies of the peignoir, and late/Coffee and oranges in a sunny chair/And the green freedom of a cockatoo/Upon a rug mingle to dissipate/The holy hush of ancient sacrifice . . ."*

With beautiful measured meter and the crackle of vivid words, this poetry offers old paganism in a new form, with sensual pleasures superseding "the holy hush of ancient sacrifice." But these pleasures are no more satisfying than a mirage, and when the blind—blinded by such mirages—lead the blind, both will find an abyss at the end of their way.

A DIALOG WITH WALLACE STEVENS

I

REWRITING "THE SNOW MAN"

One must have the mind of spring
To regard the leaves and boughs
Of the dogwood tree in bloom;

And have known Love a long time
To clearly behold the redbuds ablaze with buds,
The forsythias abloom in distant glitter

Of the April sun, and be forever mindful
Of the joy in the sound of the wind,
In the sound of many leaves,

Which is the sound of Love,
Full of the same wind
That is blowing everywhere.

For the listener who listens to Love
And that Something within himself,
Beholds the All that forever Is.

II

REWRITING "NOT IDEAS ABOUT THE THING BUT THE THING ITSELF"

At the earliest beginning of spring,
In March, a distant call from inside
As though it were a sound from outside.

He knew that he heard it,
Like a bird's call at daylight or before
In the early March wind.

The sun was rising at six,
But it was not the call of the sun
That he heard.

It was not from particle to particle
In the vast universe of matter,
Dealing only with externals.

That distant Call—it was
The first call of the Universal Muse
Over and beyond the colossal sun.

Surrounded by its Choral Rings,
Ever-present and near, it contained
The whole knowledge of reality.

III

REWRITING "OF MERE BEING"

The Word at the end of the mind
Beyond the last thought, rises
In the unrecorded distance.

An eternal rhyme
Embraces the Word with human meaning,
With human feeling, a sacred song.

You know then that is the reason
That makes us happy or unhappy.
The Word Is. Its Rhythms Sing.

The Word lives everywhere through all Space.
Poetry moves slowly in its branches,
Its rhythms in tune with Universal Time.

AS SERVANT TO THE SOURCE

To those
Who have the faith and listen intently
There is no mystery to the poetic tone.
It is everywhere throughout the Universe.
It lives
Outside the realm of magic wand or superstition.
No genius
Can claim it for his own.
It had its origin
Within the depths of Being
Where all creation first began.
It can touch
The uniqueness of an individual soul
And send it forth
To serve or sacrifice,
To find its place in all creation
In harmony with the rhythms of the planets,
Their solar systems and galaxies—
A faithful servant
To its original source:
The Love
That governs the Universe.

DANTE'S VISION: ONE OF
THE RARE MOMENTS

"The term *vision* describes that complex of personal
outlook and style and grasp of wide significance which
characterizes the work of a Dante. . . . It means having
discovered some source of inner coherence . . . "

Judson Jerome

Readers will perhaps recognize my poem, "A Love to Share,"
as an outgrowth of Dante's sublime work, *The Divine Comedy.* This
more formal poem may seem out of context here alongside the
ballads and free verse musings on life in Northwest Arkansas.
However, it is very much in context with my own story, for the
experience (which I described in my first book, *Along Sager Creek,*)
that opened up a new life for me in poetry happened upon my first
reading of the last cantos in "The Paradiso."

My well-worn edition of "The Paradiso," translated by John
Ciardi, carries the subtitle: "Dante's ultimate vision of universal
harmony and eternal salvation." I recognize this vision as one of
those rare moments in poetry and in life—a sudden awareness in
time when all that is past, all that is present, and all that is future
becomes as one in that sudden flash. In that moment, the physical
and spiritual worlds unite, and the way opens for individuals to
become unified within themselves. For six hundred years Dante's
words have shone their clear light upon troubled men looking for
the key to inner harmony:

> Like a geometer wholly dedicated
>   to squaring the circle, but who cannot find,
>   think as he may, the principle indicated—
>
> So did I study the supernal face.
>   I yearned to know just how our image merges
>   into that circle, and how it there finds place;
>
> but mine were not the wings for such a flight.
>   Yet, as I wished, the truth I wished for came
>   cleaving my mind in a great flash of light.

Here my powers rest from their high fantasy,
    but already I could feel my being turned—
    instinct and intellect balanced equally

as in a wheel whose motion nothing jars—
by the Love that moves the Sun and the other stars.

Since the time this light first shone on me, I have found a synthesis within myself where the physical and spiritual worlds are united and balanced—my opposites harmonized by the Love that moves the sun and other stars. Thus, I have felt free to use abstract words in my poem such as "Love Divine," "Sacred Muse," and "Soul." Many writers in this age would rather be found dead than suffer the embarrassment of employing such words in their poetry! We are instructed today to shun the use of abstract words, to deal only with the concrete.

This is all right as a matter of technique, but, unfortunately, this stylistic trend has led to the rejection of abstract truths which *are* Reality, towering above the concretes of our small world. The trend has encouraged both writers and readers to accept the physical, materialistic world as the only reality. However, as a critic has pointed out in *The New Criterion,* "In refusing to acknowledge the reality of any experience that is not scientifically provable, the scientific world view has condemned much that is vital to culture and creative growth."

Suzi Gablik continues, "To see things in this alienating way may be the particular compulsion of the modern Western mentality, but it does not necessarily reflect the way things really are."

I prefer to write of things as they really are! *O Sacred Muse, I thank you for your care/That brought First Things to me in poetry./ Your presence in my life made me aware/Of my own place and sense of destiny.*

118

A LOVE TO SHARE

I

O Love Divine: The perfect and all wise,
    Be the author and the master of my muse
    And cause my opposites to harmonize.

Your unseen hands I will forever choose
    To guide me where the scenes of love are shown
    And cast my eyes on everlasting views;

Each one to sink into my marrow-bone
    To dance and play and strike the sacred bars
    And keep alive the ever joyful tone

"Through Love that moves the Sun and other stars,
    Pronouncing all my inner thoughts aloud,
    As in a wheel whose motion nothing jars."*

*Dante Alighieri, *The Paradiso,* Canto **XXXIII**, transl. John Ciardi

II

I go to greet the morning, joy-endowed,
    I hear a mockingbird announce the dawn
    And see the sun's rays on a distant cloud.

I watch two robins hop across the lawn
    With thoughts of building in a nearby tree,
    Since all the signs of sleet and snow are gone.

I hold communion where I love to be,
    Beneath a maple or a sycamore
    With nature and my world in harmony.

I store each sight and sound forevermore,
    Deep, deep within my inner consciousness
    To build new rhythms in my sacred lore.

I observe the sky in all its vastness,
I am mindful of the sun at high noon,
I feel the earth in all its solidness.

Like bride and bridegroom on their honeymoon,
Each blossom has a special thing to say,
While tender breezes play the perfect tune.

And all is well when Love has ruled the day,
A joyful kind of music to unwind,
When thoughtful minds have found the steadfast way:

To hold to unity of heart and mind—
Each hill to valley, each valley to hill,
Each man to man—a joy to all mankind.

There is a time to listen and be still
And know the secret of the Universe
As Dante did, and be guided by God's Will:

God's Will and man's so wedded into verse
By Love that governs will and can be told
In simple words so all can now converse.

The laws of nature and God's law enfold
The testaments joined by a sacred birth
To tie the old with new and new with old.

The all is measured by a sacred worth,
God's love of man assembled in all space
For man to seek and find upon this earth.

III

Once again I walk out on my landscape
(It is autumn and frost hangs in the air)
In search of words to mold my thoughts in shape.

I feel a common worth while standing there
    Among the sassafras and sycamore,
    The redbud, dogwood, and oak everywhere.

O Sacred Muse, come let my mind explore
    The unknown continent within my soul
    And speak in words that sound forevermore.

And let my parts be blended in the whole
    With peace and brotherhood my greatest aim
    And Love that moves the Universe my goal.

It's harvest time and all the leaves aflame,
    The nuts and fruits and vegetables in stow;
    With happy sounds let all my words proclaim

That Love and knowledge in one stream can flow,
    Each to each without a harsh or grating sound,
    And in an instant set my heart aglow.

As all leaves within one tree are bound,
    All spirits to one root are unified,
    Alive and stabilized in solid ground.

IV

And now it's spring again on my hillside,
    Once more I celebrate the long ago
    And laud the first three days of Whitsuntide,

For the fear of death that plagues men so
    Is gone and resurrection's in the air
    And all the gladness vessels overflow.

New crops are seeded in the ground with care
    In expectation of a harvest time
    With all the bounty of the earth to share.

O Love Divine: Pray place my life in rhyme,
　　Accent the syllables to sing along
　　And link me with all time outside of Time.

Please keep me ever conscious of a song
　　In harmony with the Eternal Face
　　To guide my path and make my spirit strong.

Make me an honored member of the race
　　With new thought and feeling to explore,
　　So with the whole of things I can embrace.

And now my opposites are joined, and more;
　　It was your Love that came to rectify
　　My life and make it safe forevermore.

In joy I write these words to testify
　　For in your Name I entertained a prayer
　　That caused my self and soul to unify.

O Sacred Muse! I thank you for your care
　　That brought First Things to me in poetry.
　　Your presence in my life made me aware
Of my own place and sense of destiny.

STILL TRAVELING

We asked how far
It was to Shiloh, as if we'd stopped to ask.—He didn't know,
he'd never been on through: And waited, skyeyed, for us
to go.

Edsel Ford

Still traveling, I realize that reality exists beyond anything my five senses can experience. To say "What is real is rational and what is rational is real" is to debase reality and limit it to the mind of man. In poetry I am discovering a reality by which I am continually surprised, that resides outside the hemispheres of this world. I have used a blue guitar as a metaphor to describe this reality—not the blue of depression, but a creative blue, the pure color of a clear sky, as out of the blue, suddenly and unexpectedly, as of the unknown. The guitar, for me, expresses harmony in the Universe. Everyone possesses a blue guitar. It is their uniqueness, their potential of love and harmony with other selves.

I have looked at the world as a scientist and stood outside nature and observed and dealt in numbers. I have also been a poet, standing inside nature in tall oak trees, in dogwood blooms, in Ozark streams, inside hills and valleys, using the alphabet to speak in metaphor and simile about another hemisphere, and in all this I am continually revitalized and made whole.

I have discovered myself to be a person, unique and individual, nourishing a mind and soul, possessing a conscious and an unconscious being, capable of communicating with the collective unconscious in Universal Time, housed in a body in nature, in local time and space—a member of the human landscape, capable of communicating with its needs and thinking of its welfare.

Two worlds to conquer and unite: one a problem, one a mystery; one structured, one unstructured. In this life a journey never ended . . .

Acknowledgements

Once again I want to express my appreciation to Gloria Okes Perkins for the creative vision and skillful editing she brings to all my work. Our meeting of minds on the major themes is very helpful, and her criticism serves to lead me on to further inspiration.

I would also like to express my gratitude to *Voices International* where the poems "I Belong" and "Bridges and Building Blocks" first appeared, and to the *Arkansas Democrat* where the poems "The Great Moment" and "In the Spirit of Socrates" first appeared.

And I thank Troy Anderson, a friend and native of Siloam Springs, for the cover painting which so beautifully depicts my "Ozark Odyssey" and for the line drawings that appear on the endsheets and in the book.

TROY ANDERSON, an artist of Cherokee ancestry, paints and sculpts to preserve the folklore and history of the American Indian. His most recent awards come from the SWAIA Indian Market, Santa Fe, New Mexico; the Five Civilized Tribes Museum, Muskogee, Oklahoma; and the grand award painting from the Muxeum of the Cherokee Indian, Cherokee, North Carolina. He is currently president of The American Indian and Cowboy Artists.

GLORIA OKES PERKINS, a professional writer and poet, has won numerous awards in poetry including Arkansas's LaSalle Tricentennial Commission Award, the Grand Prize from the Poetry Society of Arizona, and the Edgar Allan Poe Memorial Award from the Poetry Society of Virginia. She is frequently called upon as a poetry critic and serves as the annual Director of the Springdale Poets and Writers Conference. She is presently writing a book for Zondervan Publishing House.

If you have enjoyed this Arkansas book
from August House, Inc., publishers,
write for our full list of 47 Arkansas books
and records. Please enclose $2 to cover
mailing and handling costs.

August House, Inc., publishers
Post Office Box 3223
Little Rock, Arkansas 72203-3223